MILITARY POLICE: ASSISTING IN SECURING THE UNITED STATES SOUTHERN BORDER

Security along the 2,000 miles of the United States southern border with Mexico is of grave concern. There are two reasons for this, the first of which is the illicit drug trade. This criminal industry, conducted by Mexican drug trafficking organizations (DTOs), has lead to an unacceptable level of violence within Mexico which has subsequently led to an increasingly lawless environment creating instability within that country. Accompanying the drug related violence in Mexico is an ever increasing threat of violence directed towards U.S. citizens both within Mexico and within the United States. Another result of the illicit drug trade is the flow of vast amounts of illegal drugs into the U.S. with all the associated ills that go with it.

The second reason security along the southern border is a concern is the inability to secure that portion of the U.S. border from entry by unknown persons. This problem is clearly demonstrated by illegal access being gained by a significant number of persons seeking work within the U.S. to include a large number of other than Mexicans (OTMS). This creates a condition whereby anyone, regardless of their intentions, could gain access into the country undetected. Together these two conditions constitute real and dangerous threats to the U.S. and make securing the southern border a national security priority.

The purpose of this paper is to suggest a way to help mitigate, not to solve, these threats with the end being defined as a reduction in the flow of illegal drugs and tighter control over who crosses our southern border. To do this I will first demonstrate that there is a serious problem by framing the environment with regards to the threats identified above. This paper will not analyze these threats in great detail but instead clearly demonstrate the scope of the threat and how they pose a real risk to the security of the United States. The way I propose to help mitigate the threat is by increasing the security forces along the southern border. The means I propose to do this is through the use of active duty military forces in a more robust role as part of the total interagency effort. More specifically, I propose that the active forces that would be best for this task are Army Military Police (MPs). I will demonstrate why MPs are the optimal choice by examining training, capabilities and culture. I will also suggest a simple model for their employment and look at associated constraints and risks. Lastly I will examine the basic question of would this proposal achieve the desired end by discussing the feasibility, acceptability and suitability of such an action.

Scope of the Threat – Illicit Drugs and Illegal Aliens

Fundamentally the threat posed to the United States is caused by two related conditions. First is the very lucrative trade between Mexico and the U.S. in illicit drugs with accompanying ill effects. Second is the ability for large numbers of persons to move into the U.S. without detection if they so desire. There are a myriad of studies illustrating that these conditions are a problem and are creating an increasingly unstable and dangerous situation along our southern border. That data and accompanying analysis could easily fill a small book so I will summarize and highlight what I feel is the most relevant.

Illicit Drug Trade

The National Drug Threat Assessment 2011 produced by the Department of Justice unequivocally states that illicit drugs continue to present a challenging threat to the United States.[1] This threat is created by the violence generated by the drug trade

2

and by the harm caused to American society by drug use. Money is the driving factor behind both of these issues. The illicit drug market is incredibly lucrative generating between 19 and 39 billion dollars annually with demand rising for all major drugs except cocaine, which has remained stable since 2007.[2] Most illicit drugs are moved into the U.S. overland across the southern border. In fact, the amount moved across the southern border greatly exceeds all other routes combined with 96% of marijuana seizures, 80% of methamphetamine seizures, 64% of cocaine seizures and 58% of heroin seizures occurring in that region.[3] Mexican DTOs dominate this trade controlling supply, trafficking and wholesale distribution.[4] Control of the smuggling routes is a key factor enabling distribution - controlling the routes equals control of distribution and thereby a greater share of the billions of dollars to be made. This situation has created a hyper-competitive environment. This hyper-competitive environment is not marked by intense advertising and pricing wars but by violence – brutal violence in the form of assassinations, mass killings and torture.

Violence is generated by competition among Mexico's seven different, major drug cartels. At its core this violence is created by inter and intra cartel fighting for control of drug trafficking routes and greater shares of the drug trade. Another element that contributes is the attempts being made by authorities to combat the DTOs. Drug related violence is largely directed at people with ties to DTOs however persons not related to DTOs are also suffering such as migrants who refused to act as drug carrying "mules", members of the press, innocent bystanders and anyone who refuses to cooperate with a DTO for any reason. Many deaths are brutal killings conducted to intimidate and in retaliation for disobedience or resistance to DTO rule. Violence is also used as a tool within organizations to strengthen leadership and impose discipline. Violence has taken the form of massacres, the killing and disappearance of Mexican journalists, the use of torture and even car bombings which has raised concerns that DTOs may be adopting techniques used by insurgents and terrorists.[5] Alarmingly DTOs are believed to be also targeting Mexican government officials. This included, in 2010, 12 Mexican mayors and a gubernatorial candidate in July of 2010.[6] Since 2006 when President Calderon declared war on DTOs until the middle of 2011 an estimated 30,000 plus Mexicans have lost their lives to drug related violence.[7] In addition to the killings and torture, kidnappings by DTOs are also becoming common with over one thousand kidnappings now reported annually with many times that number suspected.

In addition to the violence another ill effect of the drug trade that helps to enable the violence is weapons and money smuggling into Mexico from the United States. Drug sales are conducted primarily in cash which leads to an estimated 20 to 25 billion dollars moving from the U.S. back across the border into Mexico.[8] Flowing with the money are illegal weapons. A U.S. Senate report entitled, "Halting US Firearms Trafficking to Mexico", highlights statistics showing that up to 70% of firearms recovered from Mexican crime scenes could be traced to having originated in the United States.[9]

Illicit Drug Trade Effects on Mexico

The effects of the violence on Mexican society are widespread and serious. One of the more serious problems is the negative effect on the Mexican economy. Violence along the border creates instability which has a direct economic impact to Mexico not only through the cost of trying to fight DTOs but also the loss of potential industry and jobs along the border and direct investment to grow industry. According to the investment firm Bulltick Capital Markets, between 2006 and 2011 the war against drugs

4

has cost Mexico 120 billion dollars in security spending and lost investments.[10] DTOs are also using violence against Mexican industry. As an example the state-owned petroleum company, Pemex has reportedly been a repeated target of kidnappings and theft by DTOs.[11] Despite these problems the Mexican economy actually grew by 5.'% in 2011 and there has not been a flood of companies fleeing Mexico for safety reasons. However, security is a significant concern. Most experts who are monitoring the Mexican economy are seeing no immediate signs that large companies are going to pull out of Mexico. However some investments have been put on hold and prior to investing in Mexico many companies are looking harder and harder at their exposure to risk.[2]

In addition to negative economic effects the drug war has an even more serious consequence – the direct threat to the legitimacy of the Mexican government. Violence has created a condition of lawlessness in some parts of the country leading to deteriorating social conditions and an inability for Mexico to police their side of the border. There is no doubt that DTO ideology is all about profit; however their activities are successfully challenging the Mexican government and has raised serious concerns about Mexico's stability and ability to exercise sovereignty. President Calderon himself stated that DTO initiated violence presented, "a challenge to the state, an attempt to replace the state."[13] This lack of control is highlighted by several facts. One is that cartels are imposing their influence on local governments throughout the country. A study prepared for the Mexican Senate entitled, "Municipal Government and Organized Crime" released in August 2010 found that 8% of all municipalities are completely under control of organized crime while a further 63% are infiltrated and influenced by organized crime.[14] Shockingly the study found these criminal organizations often operated with logistical support from corrupt municipal police and politicians.[15] The same report also declared that DTOs have also exerted control over local businesses. A further indication of the erosion of government legitimacy are recent opinion polls showing that public support for the current Mexican government war on drugs is declining.

Illicit Drug Trade Effects on the United States

The negative effects of the drug trade on the U.S. are numerous. One of these is the negative economic impacts in the form of lost productivity and especially the money spent by states on rehabilitation, prevention and in particularly incarceration. In 2007, the estimated cost of illicit drug use to U.S. society was more than 193 billion dollars.[16] Statistics also show a strong correlation between drug use and criminal activity. In ten cities monitored across the U.S. 60% of all persons arrested tested positive for drug use.[17]

Violence is also a grave concern as violence perpetrated against Americans living within Mexico is on the rise. The U.S. Department of States claims that the first six months of 2011 were the most deadly for U.S. citizens in Mexico out of the past eight years.[18] Some of this violence can be attributed to simple criminal acts. However the link with growing cartel related violence is indisputable. A more serious problem may be spillover violence taking place within the U.S. itself. Currently, the U.S. government does not recognize spillover violence as a significant issue. However whether or not this is an issue may depend on how the question is asked. As currently reported spillover violence excludes trafficker-on-trafficker violence and counts only as violence perpetrated against civilians and government entities.[19] This is a very narrow definition of what may actually be constituting spillover violence. If actual trafficker-on-trafficker violence is counted then there is obviously violence being committed in the U.S. directly linked to DTOs. Reports by local law enforcement agencies reinforce the case for spillover violence. Of note, in June 2011 there was a report that U.S. law enforcement officials in Hidalgo county Texas received heavy weapons fire from within Mexico as they tried to interdict a load of drugs crossing the border.[20] This is an example of the increasing concerns by local law enforcement organizations, particularly Sherriff departments along the Texas, Mexican border who claim that they are now experiencing murders and higher crime as a result of DTOs.[21]

Kidnappings are another type of violence DTOs may by committing within the United States. The Department of Justice's National Drug Threat Assessment 2010 states there were 267 kidnappings in Phoenix in 2009 and 299 in 2008 with the victims usually having a connection to either human smuggling groups or drug traffickers.[22]

Another area of concern is the relationship DTOs have formed with U.S. street gangs, prison gangs and outlaw motorcycle groups (OMGs). In 2010 it was reported that 15 U.S. gangs were collaborating with Mexican DTOs. These groups are normally the organizations conducting the retail portion of the drug trade but are now also becoming increasingly involved in protection and enforcement operations for DTOs. Gang violence associated with the drug trade within the U.S. is a problem as gangs are also fighting for their share of this trade. Unfortunately the situation will likely get worse as it is projected that collaboration between gangs and DTOs will continue to increase.[23]

Current Efforts to Combat Illicit Drugs

Despite a tremendous amount of resources employed to fight the issues associated with the illicit drug trade, problems continue and are arguably getting worse in some instances. In Mexico the new Calderon administration in 2006 declared a war on drugs and the DTOs. To fight this war the Mexican government first deployed thousands of federal police to DTO strongholds. This proved to be largely unsuccessful and was soon followed by the deployment of up to 50,000 Mexican military personnel.[24] The strategy used by federal police and the military has been to target DTO leadership and organizational structure.[25] This strategy has proven somewhat successful as numerous leaders within DTOs have been either killed or captured. Another action taken by the Mexican government is that it has pursued a policy of willing cooperation with the U.S. joining in the Meridan Initiative, a 1.5 billion dollar program to expand cooperation bilaterally and regionally by providing resources and training to Mexican forces engaged in the counter drug effort.[26] Lastly, the Calderon administration is undertaking efforts to reduce corruption within the federal police force by reforming the judicial system which has proven to be ineffective and riddled with corruption itself.

These efforts by the Mexican government have met with some success especially with the targeting, capturing and killing of DTO leadership. However, there are fears that little real positive effect has been achieved and some belief that Mexico's war on drugs is proving to be futile altogether. Critics claim that any attempts at progress has been slowed and hampered by several problems. First, the strong response from the Mexican government is one factor in the increased violence as DTOs fight back in response. Second, even as DTO leadership has been arrested or killed the organizations themselves have proven very resilient by becoming more adaptive, less vertical in organizational structure and by becoming multi-nodal. Other problems cited include the fact that the Police are generally viewed as corrupt, brutal and susceptible to bribes despite purges of senior police leadership and intensive retraining efforts. As recently as August 2010 a purge of the federal police force was conducted and resulted in more than 3,000 officers being fired for being corrupt.[27]

Even the Mexican military is facing problems. Ever since becoming involved in the crackdown on DTOs the Mexican Army has been continually charged with human rights violations to include rape, killings, disappearances and torture. As recently as 2010 there were over 1,200 human rights complaints against the Army.[28] Another problem that the Army faces is a very high desertion rate, particularly among soldiers sent to fight the DTOs.[29]

Exacerbating the problems with the security forces is the lack of effective rule of law highlighted by a judicial system that is ineffective and corrupt itself. A recent study has found that of all the numerous cases brought before Mexican courts the conviction rate is only around one percent with known criminals routinely being released.[30]

The bottom line for Mexico is that violence is increasing with no foreseeable end in sight. Additionally, Mexico will continue to be the gateway for most illegal drugs entering the U.S. with the availability of most of those drugs increasing. Lastly the flow of cash and illegal weapons into Mexico continues. In combating these problems Mexican security forces have proven unable to control or improve security along the southern border and within areas controlled by cartels.

The United States has also put a great deal of resources into combating the flow of drugs, cash and weapons also with mixed results. Efforts have included the increase in the number of federal agents along the border, the employment of the National Guard by Presidents Bush and Obama, the increased use of technology such as unmanned aerial vehicles (UAVs) run by the Customs and Border Patrol, balloons with cameras looking down on the border and equipment and training assistance provided by the Department of Defense (DOD) through US Northern Command (USNORTHCOM). The U.S. government also cooperates closely with Mexican authorities to interdict, share intelligence, target and prosecute DTO members. Lastly, the U.S. is in the process of finishing 670 miles of fence along the border to help prevent uncontrolled access.

These efforts have achieved some notable successes such as the increase in the amount of drugs seized, the amount of money and weapons found flowing back across the border and the arrest and extradition by Mexico to the U.S. of DTO leadership. However, as noted by some of the statistics cited above, problems still persists and are growing worse. Additional evidence for the lack of success includes recent reports that the targeting of DTO leadership is having no significant effect and that the border fence is not as effective as hoped. There appears to be no shortage of ways to get past the fence from simple scaling with ladders to cutting with blowtorches and hacksaws and even knocking down vehicle barriers and constructing fake ones made out of cardboard.[31] DTOs even have invented and routinely use methods to breach the fence such as specially designed trucks that use ramps to allow other vehicles to cross, the increased use of tunnels, use of ultra-light aircraft in addition to the continued successful technique of utilizing commercial and non-commercial traffic to smuggle drugs at points of entry.[32] The inescapable conclusion is that despite their efforts the U.S. government has been unable to sufficiently hinder the flow of illicit drugs and the movement of cash and illegal weapons across our borders.

Inability to Secure Border against Illegal Aliens

The inability to control access into the U.S. by persons desiring entry, for whatever reason, presents another significant security threat to our nation. This is despite the fact that there has been some recent success in this area with the number of illegal immigrants being caught declining. In fact, the Department of Homeland Security currently reports that Customs and Border Patrol (CBP) apprehensions have decline 61% from 1,189,000 in 2005 to 463,000 in 2010.[33] Of those apprehensions 97 % occurred along the southern border with a majority of those persons, 86%, hailing from Mexico.[34]

The decline in the number of illegal aliens apprehended is impressive, however the numbers still are an indicator of the seriousness of the threat. Of particular concern are the fourteen percent of illegal aliens apprehended not originating in Mexico who fall into the category of other than Mexican (OTMS). While a good portion of OTMS hail from Central American a significant number come from countries all over the world to include those hostile to the United States. A report from Judicial Watch cites figures they received in response to a Freedom of Information Act request which showed that in 2010, 59,017 OTMS were apprehended.[35] Of those, 663 were from Special Interest Countries such as Cuba, Iran, Syria, Sudan, Somalia, Afghanistan, Pakistan, Saudi Arabia and Yemen.[36] What is even more alarming is that the Customs and Border Patrol estimates that only one out of every four illegal aliens is apprehended. If that were the case then the actual number of illegal aliens in 2010 crossing into the U.S. would be closer to 1,852,000 with 236,000 OTMS and of those 2,652 are from special interest countries. This movement of illegal immigrants clearly indicates near freedom of access to the U.S. from Mexico. In today's environment of transnational terrorism that is simply unacceptable.

Current US Border Security

Security along the southern border is currently conducted by a dizzying array of agencies and task forces with multiple responsibilities. The Department of Homeland Security (DHS) has been given overall responsibility for border security. DHS primarily tries to accomplish this through the Customs and Border Patrol (CBP), Immigration and Customs Enforcement (ICE) and the Transportation Security Administration (TSA). CBP is responsible for patrolling the border and inspection of persons and vehicles entering the country. The ICE is responsible for customs and immigration inspections, alien detention and deportation and air and sea interdiction. TSA is responsible for protection of air, sea and rail transportation systems within the United States. These operations are carried out all along the southern border with emphasis on high traffic points of entry. The Department of Defense supports these and other federal agencies through Joint Task Force-North (JTF-North) which was established by the USNORTHCOM. JTF-North has been authorized by Congress to loan equipment, move law enforcement personnel and conduct some detection and reconnaissance activity outside of U.S. borders in support of these agencies.

Interagency coordination for border security is conducted primarily through two different task forces. The first of this is the Organized Crime Drug Enforcement Task Force (OCDEF). The OCDEF focuses primarily on drug trafficking and smuggling. The second task force is the Border Enforcement Security Task Force (BEST) which also focus on drug crimes as well as other crimes in the border region to include targeting weapons leaving the United States. Both task forces bring together not only the various organizations within DHS but also the Justice Department and the Bureau of Alcohol Tobacco and Firearms.

Shortcomings

As shown above current U.S. and Mexican policy and efforts are not working. Non-U.S. citizens have continued undocumented access into the country and a significant portion of this population is from countries other than Mexico to include the Middle East. Violence has not decreased and Mexico cannot claim to control areas dominated by DTOs. The threat to U.S. citizens along the border has not decreased and may actually be worse and illegal drugs continue to flow into the United States. Simply put the threat is real and is not diminishing.

A Way to Mitigate

In today's environment the threats presented above create risks that the U.S. Government should not be willing to take. One of the issues associated with combating these threats is the sheer size of the problem and the limited resources available. One way to achieve the end is to therefore provide more resources to secure the border to include more people and more equipment. The means I propose to do this with is to deploy active duty military forces, primarily ground forces, to assist in securing the southern border as part of the interagency effort. I propose that the optimal means to be used in accomplishing this are U.S. Army Military Police Soldiers utilized in functional military police organizations.

Of all the active duty forces available why employ Military Police (MPs)? There are several key reasons why I propose this. MPs are Sold ers who have proven proficiency in conducting various war fighting missions around the globe. However at their heart MPs are police, trained and experienced in executing law and order (L&O) operations. In performing this function MPs routinely perform typical policing tasks such as community patrolling, responding to calls for assistance as well as perform traffic operations, criminal investigations and even providing support to customs operations while deployed overseas.[37] Military police have continuous experience performing these types of mission which they conduct primarily within Army communities and within Army organizations who they may deploy with. In the last ten years MPs have also been called upon to assist in training other nations' police forces in both Iraq and Afghanistan.

As policemen MPs are trained, experienced and have unique skills and mind sets not possessed by other military forces. This is a result of both the training received by MPs and of the conditions they routinely operate in. One result of this training and experience is the approach MPs learn to use when conducting their L&O mission. This approach emphasizes: rapid and accurate assessment of the environment, focusing on the criminal dimension, effective interpersonal communication skills, critical thinking and problem solving to establish control and de-escalate incidents, and lastly the ability to rapidly identify threats and choose the application of appropriate force options (from verbal persuasion to lethal force) necessary to control the environment.[38] Another benefit of the conditions MPs routinely work in is that they become highly suited for interacting with both military and civilian populations. The bottom line is that through training and the execution of L&O operations MPs reinforce a unique mindset and gain critical interpersonal and technical policing skills which give them a set of capabilities setting them apart from other Soldiers.

Another characteristic is that from very early in their careers MPs often are required to work alone without immediate supervision. This environment helps to create confident and proficient police who are used to dealing with complex situations and a variety of people from senior ranking military to ordinary civilians. These skills and attributes also provide another advantage for MPs. While other military units may be unacceptable to local populations due to their perceived combat functions, MPs can be seen as less threatening and more acceptable.

Another advantage MPs have is that they routinely work with other law enforcement agencies outside of the U.S. military. MPs conducting L&O on installations interact and work with local and state law enforcement agencies on an almost daily basis. In addition, MP leaders work and coordinate with local, state and federal agencies as they perform their mission to protect Army installations against crime and terrorism.

The environment MPs would be required to work in along the southern border would be complex and potentially very visible to public scrutiny. It would require MPs to work closely with other government agencies and also require them to interact with the American public. It would put them in a position where their unique skills would not only be beneficial but also completely necessary. This is why MPs would be the optimal military force to assist with securing the southern border.

Aside from the unique skills and mindset of the MP Soldier one other Military Police capability must be mentioned. MP organizations are expeditionary, possessing a robust capability to operate in austere environments for extended periods of time. MP organizations down to the company level have been designed specifically to operate independently. While this capability is resident in many military organizations the thing that sets MPs apart is their training and capacity to operate independently as small organizations. The basic MP formation is the three person team operating out of a vehicle and trained and equipped to conduct MP missions alone. MPs are organized to operate independently up to company size elements. This capability was specifically designed so that MPs could be used over large portions of terrain supporting larger Army formations.

MP Employment Model

Just throwing MPs at the security problem along the southern border would not necessarily help unless employed correctly to maximize their capabilities. A proposed model to accomplish this task looks like this:

- An MP brigade (BDE) headquarters deploys with two subordinate MP battalions each with four subordinate MP companies. This would provide a force of approximately 1625 total military personnel and a total of 336 MP three person teams. Doctrinally this would allow the BDE to assist with securing approximately 500 km of border.[39] This of course is based partly on the terrain and other factors such as employing more MPs in areas of greater risk but this figure does provide an idea of what such a force could do.

- MP forces would deploy primarily along remote and more inaccessible portions of the border where MP capabilities could best be used. The southern border of Arizona is a prime example where open deserts dominate and there are preferred areas where smuggling occurs due to terrain features.

- Although exceptionally capable, in order to ensure this organization succeeded in their mission the MP BDE would have to be given some enablers to further enhance their capabilities. Suggested enablers include the addition of signal assets to provide more robust communications architecture and medical personnel at the brigade and battalion level to provide adequate health care to the Soldiers and any civilians working with them. Two other suggestions would be to include engineer assets that could assist with meeting simple infrastructure requirements and some air defense assets, particularly radar, to assist with identifying ultra light and other aircraft used to smuggle drugs and people across the border. Additional augmentation might be needed at the brigade and battalion staff levels to assist with the planning and tracking of operations and to fulfill any technical responsibilities not resident in the brigade headquarters.

- This organization would also require interagency support from subject matter experts and liaisons in order to facilitate coordination and ensure specific tasks are handled by the appropriate agency. Representatives from the CBP would be necessary to help plan operations, coordinate and deconflict with other agency forces and to provide subject matter expertise. At the tactical level, MP companies would need to have the ability to coordinate with and reach back to the interagency world as well. Small interagency teams imbedded with companies could provide this resource. These teams could be located at the company headquarters and then moved to areas whenever and wherever they were needed.

- To empower military forces to accomplish their mission they will be given an expanded role to directly interdict, detain and hold illegal immigrants. Additionally, the military will actively interdict drug flow through identification of routes, detention of suspected drug traffickers and searches of vehicles and non-U.S. citizens. In order to perform these missions it is clear that active

17

MPs would need to be empowered by expanding current military authority which would require U.S. Congressional approval.

Benefits

One obvious benefit is that the employment of this MP task force provides more resources to combat the threats identified. This could free up federal and state enforcement agency manpower allowing them to concentrate on points of entry, transportation corridors and more populated areas. Another benefit is that the MP task force would be flexible and could conceivably deploy to where they were needed for however long they were needed. Mexican DTOs have proven very adaptive to changing border conditions so the ability to apply this type of flexible response could adversely impact that capability. Ultimately if successful in its mission MPs would have assisted in combating the threats discussed above.

Risk

There are several valid and important risks that accompany this proposal. First, there is a real risk that success will actually lead to more violence and even invite violence onto the U.S. side of the border. One of the reasons that drug related violence has climbed in Mexico since 2006 is that the Mexican government began to more rigorously fight the DTOs with security forces. If the DTOs began to see their profits significantly impacted they might decide to direct attacks against U.S. security forces to include MPs. By bringing heightened violence to the U.S. side of the border they could hope to persuade U.S. policy makers and their constituents that things were better before the MPs arrived.

Another risk is that this type of action could foreseeably alienate Mexico from the U.S. and actually hurt efforts to secure the border. Mexico has always been wary of

U.S. intentions and outside interference partly because of the past history between the two countries. The deployment of active military forces along the southern border could possibly be seen as a prelude to further intervention. This in turn may turn Mexico away from cooperative efforts to secure the border.

The deployment of active military along the border could pose another risk with regards to our own people. There could be backlash from Americans who feel that the military should not be employed in such a manner within the country. This sediment could weaken the will of the government and lose support for the military by the American public.

Lastly is the risk of success. If this mission were seen as a success it might create a condition where both politicians and the public come to expect active Soldiers securing the southern border. It could leave the Army with a mission with no end in sight.

Feasible Acceptable Suitable (FAS) Test

In order to help determine whether or not this proposal would work I have applied the FAS test. In applying this test I have determined the following:

- This proposal is feasible. An active duty MP forces could be deployed along the southern border. It would also be feasible to tie these forces into the current C2 provided by JTF-North under the DHS. Ground forces would need time to build supporting infrastructure from which to operate however this is not something that would prevent this option from being executed.

- The question of acceptability is a little more complicated. With the current threat and increased pressure from U.S. Border States for the Federal

Government to act, most would see this option as acceptable. However in order to be considered completely legal the U.S. Congress would have to approve the role and mission of the military. Although not insurmountable in the current environment it may prove difficult. Another issue would be the reaction of the Mexican government. Mexico has been historically very concerned about the use of U.S. military forces along their border. Although the option could be executed without Mexican support the possibility of backlash from Mexico could generate second and third order effects that must be considered and mitigated.

- This option is suitable in that it would enhance border security. However in the long term it does not address the underlying issues that create the problems and therefore long term suitability is in question. A new comprehensive drug policy that works to reduce the demand is required and to date the U.S. has not been able to accomplish this. The same problem exists with immigration policy as it has escaped several attempts to solve the issue. However in order to completely secure our borders and create conditions to do this there needs to be a new and comprehensive policy that allows for migrant workers to have access to the United States. Gaining acceptance of a comprehensive and effective drug and immigration policy may fail due to lack of consensus by policy makers.

Conclusion

In conclusion, there is clearly a threat to U.S. security along our southern border and the threat is not going away despite significant efforts by both the U.S. and Mexican governments. The threat to the U.S. is posed by the illicit drug trade from Mexico. This trade in turn is responsible for unacceptable levels of violence that is threatening the very legitimacy of the Mexican government. Loss of a legitimate government is bad for the U.S. as it could have adverse economic impacts and ead to increased violence within the U.S. itself. The drug trade also has significant social impacts for American society such as increased health care and law enforcement costs and lost productivity due to drug abuse not to mention the gang violence perpetrated due to drugs.

Another threat to the U.S. is posed by the ability of persons to cross the southern border unimpeded and unknown to U.S. authorities. This situation is especially worrisome in light of the current terrorist threat.

Efforts to curb these threats have proven elusive and one of the reasons for this is a lack of resources to tackle this very large problem. A way to help mitigate this is to deploy U.S. Army Military Police forces to the southern border. MPs are uniquely suited for such as mission through their police training and experience. While there are some risks to consider and significant political preparation and shaping to be accomplished I believe that this is a viable option. The conditions within Mexico and along our southern border are a national security threat. The role of the military is to assist with eliminating threats to the nation therefore the military should be looked at seriously to assist in this particular situation.

Endnotes

[1] U.S. Department of Justice National Drug Intelligence Center, *National Drug Threat Assessment 2011* (Washington, DC: National Drug Intelligence Center, August 2011), 1.

[2] Ibid. 2-3.

[3] Ibid. 13.

[4] Ibid. 2.

[5] June S. Beittel, Mexico's *Drug Trafficking Organizations: Source and Scope of the Rising Violence* (Washington, DC: U.S. Library of Congress, Congressional Research Service, January 7, 2011), 2.

[6] Ibid. 1.

[7] Kristin M. Finklea, William J. Krouse and Mark A. Randol, *Southwest Border Violence: Issues in Identifying and Measuring Spillover Violence* (Washington, DC: Library of Congress, Congressional Research Service, January 25, 2011), 1.

[8] June S. Beittel, Mexico's *Drug Trafficking Organizations: Source and Scope of the Rising Violence*, 21.

[9] BBC News, Latin America & Caribbean, "Q&A: Mexico's drug-related violence," BBC News Online, August 26, 2011, http://www.bbc.co.uk/news/worl-latin-america/ (accessed December 10, 2011).

[10] Michael Riley, "Mexico's Drug War Takes to the Blogosphere," Bloomberg BusinessWeek, November 9, 2011

[11] Devon Duff and Jen Rygler "Drug Trafficking, Violence and Mexico's Economic Future," Wharton School of the University of Pennsylvania, Knowledge@Wharton, *http://www.knowledge.wharton.upenn.edu*, January 26, 2011.

[12] "Mexico's Drug War Impacts Business," Wharton School of the University of Pennsylvania, Knowledge@Wharton, *http://www.knowledge.wharton.upenn.edu*, September 16, 2011.

[13] Beittel, *Mexico's Drug Trafficking Organizations: Source and Scope of the Rising Violence*, 2.

[14] Ibid. 26.

[15] Ibid.

[16] U.S. Department of Justice National Drug Intelligence Center, *National Drug Threat Assessment 2011*, 17.

[17] Ibid.

[18] Insight – Organized Crime in the Americas, "Mexican Drug Cartels and the Limits of Rational Choice," InSight Online, December 2, 2011, http://insightcrime.org/insight-latest-news/item/1922-mexican-drug-cartels-and-the-limits-of-rational-choice/ (accessed December 3, 2011).

[19] Kristin M. Finklea, William J. Krouse and Mark A. Randol, *Southwest Border Violence: Issues in Identifying and Measuring Spillover Violence*, 12.

[20] Julian Aguilar, *"Texas Police Under Cross-Border Gunfire,"* Tucson Sentinel Online, June 9, 2011, http://www.tucsonsentinel.com/nationworld/report/060911_officers_fired_on/texas-police-under-cross-border-gunfire/ (accessed December 6, 2011).

[21] Brian Bilbray and John Carter, *Broken Neighbor, Broken Border,* A Field Investigation Report of the House Immigration Reform Caucus (Washington, DC: U.S. House of Representatives, November 19 2010), 5-6.

[22] U.S. Department of Justice National Drug Intelligence Center, *National Drug Threat Assessment 2010* (Washington, DC: National Drug Intelligence Center, August 2011), 15.

[23] U.S. Department of Justice National Drug Intelligence Center, *National Drug Threat Assessment 2011,* 11.

[24] Beittel, *Mexico's Drug Trafficking Organizations: Source and Scope of the Rising Violence,* 18.

[25] Ibid.

[26] Ibid.

[27] Ibid. 19.

[28] George W. Grayson, "Threat Posed by Mounting Vigilantism In Mexico," U.S. Army War College Strategic Studies Institute Online, September 2011,19.

[29] Ibid. 20.

[30] Ibid. 26.

[31] Jacques Billeaud, *"Fence's Effectiveness Debated: $2.4 Billion Structure is far from a Cure-all for Nation's Borders,"* Richmond Times Dispatch (VA) Online, May 28, 2010, http://www.lexisnexis.com/1nacui2api/delivery/(accessed December 6, 2011).

[32] Mark Potter, "Illegal Drugs Flow Over and Under U.S. Border," MSNBC Online, October 22, 2009, http://www.msnbc.msn.com/id/33433955/ns/us_news-crime_and_courts/t/illegal-drugs-flow/ (accessed December 3, 2011).

[33] Department of Homeland Security: Office of Immigration Statistics Fact Sheet, *Apprehensions by the U.S. Border Patrol: 2005-2010* (Washington DC: Department of Homeland Security, July 2011) 1.

[34] Ibid. 2.

[35] *"Judicial Watch Obtains New Border Patrol Apprehension Statistics for Illegal Alien Smugglers and Special Interest Aliens,"* Judicial Watch Online, March 9, 2011, http://www.judicial watch.org/news/2011/mar/judicial-watch-obtains-new-border-patrol-apprehension-statistics/ (accessed December 6, 2011).

[36] Ibid.

[37] Headquarters, Department of the Army, *Military Police Operations*, FM 3-39 (Washington DC: Headquarters, Department of the Army, February 16, 2010) 3-3 - 3-4.

[38] Headquarters, Department of the Army, *Military Police Operations*, FM 3-39, 1-2.

[39] Headquarters, Department of the Army, *Military Police Operations*, FM 3-39, 1-2.